Marlys,

Enjoy the
stories from
our old house

Duane Dutt

1

Forward

I have been fascinated with the history of our first home ever since Pete Nickel started telling us stories while he was taking lumber out of the old house before it was demolished. My curiosity was peaked as I wondered about all the families who had inhabited our house. Even though I knew some stories from previous occupants, this is mainly a story of the events that occurred while we lived in the house. This book was written for my children and grandchildren. These are true stories and events from our lives written from my perspective. It was my intention to list names of people my children might remember and describe buildings that might bring back childhood memories. I purposely included stories and wonderings of past times for the sake of my grandchildren to help them understand how technology has advanced during my lifetime and also how people lived without many of the modern conveniences we take for granted today.

Dedication

This book is dedicated to my loving and patient husband, who encouraged me to write these stories in a book. His enjoyment of reading the stories and remembering the events spurred me on when I wondered if my children would even be interested in these everyday events. He also helped with remembering details and coming up with stories or events that should be included. He even provided the Florida winter trips that allowed me to concentrate on writing. So with much appreciation, I am so pleased to have my first book dedicated to the love of my life, Jim.

Just an Ordinary House

I stared into the fire. The wood crackled as it became consumed by the flames. So this was it. It was final – the end of an era. I stood watching the fire with mixed emotions. Even though I was looking to the future with excitement and my present life was full of happiness, my emotions concerning this fire were heavy with a sentimental sadness. The blaze in front of me was the final farewell to our old house – the house that had stood here through most of the century. Decades of family life had taken place in that house. I had only lived in it for five years, but there were so many memories and events that had shaped my life during the time we called that house "home".

As the fire burned I wondered about the people who built this house. I wondered if they ever thought about the future of the house. Did they wonder how many families might call it home or how many years it might stand here on this yard? I'm sure they could never have imagined all the changes that would take place during the lifetime of this building. Farming was

*done with actual horses for horsepower when
this house was built. There were no rural
electric lines and probably no water lines
running into the house when it was new. Even
though it had spanned an era of time from
horses to tractors, from ledger books to
computers, from a walk to visit the neighbors to
an overseas phone call; the time had come to
an end for its usefulness to us. I couldn't stop
wondering, though, what had happened within
these walls? Oh, if only the walls could talk.
They could tell of joys shared, heart-wrenching
decisions made, happy family gatherings, the
sadness from grief and loss of a loved one, and
the excitement of new love and new life. The
memories these walls held live on in the hearts
of the people who inhabited this dwelling – as
the memories live on in my heart. How many
new babies were born in this house, or brought
home from the hospital to this first home of
their young lives? How many hours of tears of
grief were shed as the loss of a loved one was
mourned? How much time had been spent in
prayer and praise to God here? How much*

laughter and chatter had echoed off these walls as friends and family gathered?

Not only did I not know the answers to any of these questions the first time I saw the house, but at that point in time, the questions hadn't even entered my mind. I was young and interested in seeing this house, but for me, it was just an ordinary house. At a time when many homes were inhabited by succeeding generations of the same family, this house sat empty and was now owned by a neighbor (Jim) who was not related to anyone who had formerly lived in the house. So as far as I was concerned, it was merely a house. I knew no history of the house or yard the first time I saw it, unlike Jim who grew up knowing the neighbors who had lived there.

I was only 17 at the time. Jim & I were on one of our dates that were becoming more regular all the time. He wanted to check on his pigs so we turned in the driveway that was to become so familiar to me over the next 39 years. It was a long driveway with a curve at the midway point. All I could see was the big, old barn, sitting no more than 10 feet from the driveway, hiding most of the yard. The windbreak of trees, consisting mostly of ash, elm, and cottonwood with a few mulberries thrown in, encircled the yard. As we passed the barn, sitting there as the sentinel to guard the yard, I could see a large evergreen tree, with the house partially hidden behind it. It stood much taller than the 2 story house itself.

As I was looking over the house and yard, Jim was checking to see if there were any new baby pigs in the farrowing barn. He had only been farrowing pigs for a year, and they were a precious commodity to him, even though the price had fallen and now he was selling feeder pigs for very little. When he first bought his breeding stock, the price of feeder pigs was $40 a piece – a nice profitable operation. But now they had fallen to $10 a piece and there was no money to be made, but still, every pig saved was worth $10 and he was determined to save every one. His dad, Anton, had helped him remodel one of the two chicken barns into a farrowing barn and the expensive new gilts had arrived last spring. I could tell the pride he took in his new business venture. The size of his operation, sixty sows, was a large operation at that time in our community.

Eighteen months before, in the fall of 1969, Jim had found himself in the position of making a quick decision whether to buy this 9-acre building site. He had just arrived home after a 28-month term of service with Mennonite Central Committee in Bolivia, South America. Even though his dad had written and told him of the opportunity to buy this site, he hadn't given it much consideration before Clark Fast, our neighbor, came over to see Jim the *third day he was back home in the U.S. and asked if he wanted the place. That day Jim, Anton, and Clark all came over to this building site which had been standing empty for a year already, to evaluate its usefulness. Very little time had been spent looking at the house that day – the consensus being that it was adequate as farm houses go, meaning "a farm house is a farm house". It's the other buildings that are important for the farm to survive. That certainly matched the history of this yard that had a house/ barn combination on it during the late 1800s. On that day in 1969, the attention of the three men was concentrated on the barns, as Jim was evaluating the usefulness of the whole yard. The newer, long, chicken barns were carefully evaluated to decide if they could fit into the farm business as Jim wanted to develop it. Anton was looking at these poultry barns through the eyes of a turkey farmer and could easily see that they could fit well for that purpose, but Jim was looking for hog barns and had big remodeling plans running through his mind. In the end, the decision was made, and Jim ended up with a contract for deed for*

$10,000 for a 9 ¾ acre squared off building site that sat in the middle of the quarter section of land. The contract was made with Aaron Becker (whom Clark had purchased the surrounding land from). For the first time in its history, the house was now owned by a young farmer who owned none of the farm land surrounding it.

On this, my first visit to this yard, I wasn't even aware of the history of Jim's purchase. I had been happily waiting in my boyfriend's 65 Chevy, taking in the whole yard, but especially the house, as I waited for him to finish in the barn. He came back and we were ready to leave, but I begged to see the house. How could he refuse this charmer, whom he had already decided might be the wife who moves into this house with him?

Brushing past the evergreen branches that had grown over the sidewalk, we made our way up the front porch steps. It was a small porch but so friendly, inviting one to stand by the railing and look out over the yard laid out in a circle around the yard light pole. The house sat on a hill looking down on all the other

buildings on the yard. The big, old, dairy barn
was down the hill to the north. At that time, the
barn was being used to shelter the young sows
that grazed and rutted the whole 2 acres on the
northwest end of the building site. A small, old
granary that had been partially converted to a
machine shed, with a work bench and just
enough room to park a small tractor, sat at the
bottom of the yard on the east side. Just to the
south of the granary was the old chicken barn
that housed the other set of young sows that
roamed the pasture to the east and north
covering the northeast 2 acres on the other side
of the driveway. The sows had no problem
keeping the dirt black and weed free in their
pasture that was fenced off with electric fence
wire to keep each group in their designated
pasturing area. This farm yard surely must have
had a different look when the previous owners
had dairy cattle grazing the green grass! On the
southeast side of the circular yard sat the two
newest buildings – the long chicken barns. One
was 60 feet long, running east and west; the
other was 80 feet long running north and south.
They were connected by an alley and granary

with overhead bins for feed and grain. The 60 foot long barn was the one that had been remodeled into Jim's farrowing barn. Anton had borrowed Jim $10,000 for equipment and cement and the two Dick men had worked many long hours making three rows of cement pits for the manure storage. Then they poured cement for the floor where the 33 farrowing crates would stand, with oak slats covering the pits so the manure could fall through, but the baby pigs would not. There was enough room for a driveway around the barns. On the west side of that drive sat a 3500 bushel grain bin. Just a few feet south of the house sat a two car garage with a 2 foot high wall of pink bricks on either side forming the drive into the garage. Three steps made of bricks gave easy access from the driveway in front of the garage to the sidewalk leading to the kitchen door.

As we moved into the house, I loved the front entry with the partially open staircase and dark wooden banister post with railing following the first 4 steps up until it met the wall. The entry walls were paneled, which was a popular covering in the 60s and 70s. Since this was 1971, I thought the newly remodeled room was so welcoming. It became one of my favorite rooms in the house. But I wonder now if this was the way the room was laid out when the house was built, or had it been part of the living room? A wooden door separated it from the living room, which joined the dining room with a 10 foot open archway. I loved the openness because many older houses had a living room that would be completely closed off with doors – still part of the "Sunday parlor" idea of having a special room that was used only for guests or Sundays. The living room had an old brown Berber type carpet covering the hardwood floor, while the dining room had fairly up to date linoleum. Each room had a large window – the living room window facing east, looking out over the yard, and the dining room facing west, looking toward the grove, with the backyard pasture in between. We walked down the slanted floor into the kitchen which was 8 inches lower than the dining room. There had been a door between the 2 rooms but I could see it had been taken out at some point, with no hinges remaining. This room definitely *looked like it had been added later. The kitchen was no treasure to me, and a year later when plans were being made for us to move into the house after our honeymoon, I staunchly stated that I would not use that kitchen! I thought at the time perhaps we could make the dining room into a kitchen. (Who knows what I thought we would actually do with the room that I refused to use for a kitchen!) At that point I never knew all the stories that those kitchen walls knew. I never knew how the Lord was leading a young father to touch lives of people far away and lead them into a relationship with Jesus.*

As I looked around that first night I saw the rusted steel cabinets covered with contact paper over plywood for a countertop. I saw the worn floor and the chimney that left stains running down the wall. I saw the old enamel sink with one bright spot – new faucets. There was a door from the kitchen to the outside. Since this was a farm house, all the dirty work clothes and boots would pass through this door and into the kitchen. It must have been that way for all the families who had lived in this house, although that never occurred to me on this particular night when I was seeing the layout of the house for the first time.

We turned around, and heading back through the dining room, walked down the hall to the bedroom. Off to our left was the entrance to the bathroom – another room that was not very welcoming as far as I was concerned. The walls were covered with a laminated imitation pink tile, which was pealing and not in very good condition anymore. The fixtures were all usable, but older, and the floor was well worn. I never noticed the electric heater built into the wall, that years later would provide one warm room for our baby in a cold, cold house. Thinking back now of when the house was built, surely there wasn't a bathroom in it in the early twentieth century, nor would there have been electricity and probably no running water. Was this room just part of the bedroom next to it when the house was built? I marvel to think how many times this house may have been remodeled during those years of growing conveniences.

We moved on into the bedroom and I noticed the wall of closet space that looked like it had just been added or remodeled. It made the room smaller but gave much needed storage space. I blushed when Jim mentioned that this was the "work room", but it didn't stop me from accepting a kiss from him.

Later that evening, after Jim had dropped me off at my home, I thought of that house and how life would be if we would be married and living together there. "No, Diane, dismiss that thought," I told myself. "It is far too early in the relationship to dream of a house you might live in sometime in the future."

Time passed and our relationship grew. We found we shared a deep friendship and joy of spending time with each other. We had come from similar backgrounds and realized we both appreciated the community we had grown up in and wanted to put our roots down and stay here. Our common faith in God bound us together. By the next summer we were engaged and busy working on the house. The wedding date was set for Aug. 19 and my intention was that the house would be ready to live in before we moved in so that no further remodeling would be needed. Jim and I had evaluated the house and realized that it eventually would need to be picked up and put on a new foundation since the floor was already lower on the outside edges and higher over the partial basement, creating a rounded effect to the floor. Actually the whole foundation for the house, which was made of large rocks cemented together to hold them in place, had settled, leaving the middle of the floor higher because it was over the basement which hadn't settled. The basement (or cellar, which seemed like a more appropriate word to me) was only about the size of a quarter of the house. It followed the wall of the bathroom/ bedroom and living room / entry down into the ground 7 feet and was about 7 feet wide with the other long wall under the middle of the dining room and living room, which over time was creating the rounded floors. All the walls in the cellar were made of large rocks cemented together. In some places the cement was plastered over the rocks to create an almost smooth wall. In other places the huge boulders jutted out, making me wonder how difficult it had been to put them in place so many years ago. The cement floor was cracked, and in one corner almost completely broken up, which explained why I saw salamanders so often down there that I had to be careful where I stepped. There were no windows but the light was wired to a light switch so at least I had light before I started down the open back steps. In my mind I could imagine earlier families making their way down this stairway with a lantern in hand, to fetch jars of home canned garden produce from the wooden shelves that still lined the sides of the long walls, or maybe a ham that was hanging down there to cure. Perhaps they were after some potatoes or carrots stored in this spot that was cool in summer but warm enough in winter to keep it from freezing. My little sister, Sandi, was always afraid to go down in the cellar. I wondered how many other children who had lived in this house shuddered at the thought of that dark room down under!

We also knew that a furnace should be installed, all the windows (except the dining room) needed to be replaced, and the roof would need shingling in not too many years. The house should also be sided and insulated. It was like many other rural homes in our area at that time – suffering from the lack of remodeling and updating that would have been done if the farm economy had been better during the 50s and 60s. Our goal was to spend as little as possible to make the home livable for as long as we could survive it.

Jim worked on removing the kitchen chimney. We never did understand at that point why there was a chimney with no place for a stove to be hooked in, but as he pulled it apart we could see there must have been a cook stove (that could burn wood, corn cobs, or coal for both heat and cooking) there years ago that needed that chimney. Years later we heard a wonderful story that gave us happy memories of that old leaky chimney. As my soon-to-be-husband worked on the chimney, my job was to sand the rusted cabinets and apply a coat of bright green paint (anything to make that kitchen brighter!) to the cabinets. We had also purchased two new steel cabinets (that I also painted) to add on the south wall were there hadn't been any upper cabinets. Those were happy days to be working together on the house that we would soon be living in together! We painted the kitchen and my father put a Formica counter top on top of the base cabinets (a big improvement over the plywood covered with contact paper). I guess we would use that room for a kitchen after all. Many years later, in talking with a niece of the former owners, Lori Krause, I discovered that I was not the only one who thought the kitchen was outdated. She remembers going into the kitchen as a girl and thinking it was quite old fashioned to have a pump that you pumped by hand to get water in the sink. When the kitchen was built, there was a cistern put in under it from which the pump was drawing the water. The pump had been eliminated shortly before Jim bought the house, and that's why we had new faucets in the kitchen.

In order to be able to use the front door, Jim had the large evergreen tree (that had taken over the front sidewalk) cut down.

Both of my parents helped us put up new wallpaper in the living room and dining area. There! On less than $500 my house was livable! How many times had this happened over the past 70 years? A new family moves in and they update the house to make it their own, as much as their budget will allow.

Before the wedding we purchased a living room set (quite outdated since it was from the 40's, but it was cheap - $14 for both pieces) and a bedroom set (which was much newer and included the mattress and box spring) from a household auction. My parents had recently replaced their refrigerator & stove, so they gave us their old ones. Slowly my house was getting furnished but we were still lacking a table & chairs. A used set was advertised for sale in the paper and after looking at it and liking it, it was given to us as a wedding present from my parents. Jim's parents later added a coffee table & 2 end tables as their wedding present. Now our home was ready to be lived in. I was so pleased as I looked around at this new home we would be moving into. Who would have guessed that only five years later *we would run an ad in the paper that began, "This old shack has got to go. . . . . ."*

By September 1972 we were living in what we called "our honeymoon cottage". After our wedding on August 19, we had taken a week off for the honeymoon and spent it in northern Minnesota, but that didn't mean that the honeymoon hadn't continued in our new home as more memories of the joy of young love and learning to live together flooded these walls again. Surely this was not the first honeymoon couple within the life of this house!

One of the first things we would need to really settle in would be food to make meals. I had a long grocery list as I had headed into Mountain Lake for my first grocery shopping excursion. I passed by the "Franz store", which sat on the northwest corner of the one way street, and did my first shopping in the Fairway store at the south end of the block. I later patronized the Franz store before it burned down, along with half of that block in 1975.

As I shopped, it surprised me how quickly the bill added up. The checkout lady saw my full cart and started asking questions, since I was a new face in the store. The store gave us a pound of bacon as a housewarming gift and to thank us for shopping there. Back at home, as I was trying to decide where the staples would be stored, I smiled as I placed the free bacon in the refrigerator. This was really my home and I was in charge of the kitchen. However, cooking was something I had little interest in.

Chapter 2

The smell of the fire, as we watched the old house burn, reminded me of some of the smell of my cooking from that kitchen. Some of my early meals smelled as burnt as this fire, but I gradually learned how to cook. Jim ate many meals that other men may have complained about, but he had no more interest in cooking than I did, so he said nothing. Sometimes he even complimented me on a dish that tasted good or a good meal. Slowly, I was learning.

That kitchen had many more stories to tell, only a few of which I knew. For me, the memories of driving our 65 Chevy up to the garage and unloading the groceries from our first shopping trip is still vivid in my mind. The garage was set at a 45 degree angle to the house. Aaron Becker had shared with Jim on a visit, shortly after we were moved in, of his plans to replace the kitchen with a new one and add a laundry room / entry, thus attaching the kitchen to the garage. Now we knew why the kitchen had been so unappealing – it was the next room on the remodeling list! The garage was only about 3 feet from the kitchen wall at the closest point, perhaps 10 feet apart at the back wall. That certainly would give enough room to make a nice laundry room and entry between the garage and kitchen. Perhaps there were plans to have a wash up area out there, too. As it was, there was no place to clean up before you entered the room that the food was being prepared in. During the summer, boots and dirty shirts and jackets could be taken off before entering the room. But by winter, we realized we needed someplace away from the area that we ate in to put the boots so they didn't sit outside and freeze or fill with snow. I was very certain I didn't want the manure smell in the kitchen! The landing at the top of the steps to the cellar seemed like a good spot. Nails were put in to hang barn jackets and a rug made a spot for the boots to sit. Best of all, we could close the door and keep most of the smell in that room. From there it was easy to walk around the dining room wall and into the bathroom to wash up.

The kitchen had always looked like a room that had been added later. It may have *been, but we never did talk to anyone who knew that to be a fact. It was a large room, perhaps 15' x 15'. The doorway to the dining room was on the north wall. The door to the outside was on the far north side of the east wall, with a wall heater positioned just next to it, between the outside door and a long narrow window. This window overlooked the area of the yard out towards the farrowing barn and gave me a good view of Jim coming from the barn to the house for a meal. There was plenty of room along that east wall, in front of the window, for a small table, and we found one at an auction for a few dollars that fit perfectly. This was almost always our eating area unless we had company, then we ate in the dining room. The dining room table was much more of an office area and place to sit and read the mail. Our one and only telephone was mounted to the wall, just above the heater and right beside the outside door in the kitchen. During the time that we lived in that house, we had a 'party line', meaning that there were a number of neighbors all on the same line. If you picked up the phone, you might hear someone else talking. The polite thing to do would be to hang up and wait until later, but the neighbors may not have heard you pick up the phone and sometimes a person could catch up on what is going on in the community by 'rubber necking' or listening in. Our phone ring was distinct from that of the neighbors so we would only pick up the phone when it rang our particular ring (too short rings and one long). The phone companies were already in the process of modernizing and it wasn't long before we didn't hear the neighbors' telephone rings anymore. That way, we didn't know if they were on the line or not, which gave us all a little more privacy.*

My refrigerator and stove, along with a set of cabinets (wall cabinets and floor cabinets) sat along the south wall, where the ugly chimney had been. On the west wall was a window the same size as the east window, but you wouldn't have guessed the window was that big because the sink set up against it, allowing one to only look out of the top half of the window. The view from the west window looked out over the back yard, which for many years had been the pasture area for the calves, before we moved onto the yard. We once heard Aaron Becker refer to it as the "orchard", but there were no fruit trees left by the time we moved onto the yard.

Looking around at my kitchen, I wondered how it had looked when it was new. It probably had a cook stove by the chimney on the south wall. Did it have an ice box sitting somewhere to keep the food cold? I knew there were people in this community at that time who "harvested" the ice in big chunks from a lake in winter and loaded it on wagons pulled by horses and then unloaded it into a well shaded building, stacking the ice chunks with sawdust in between to keep them from melting all summer. If there were some enterprising ice merchants, they may have made the rounds with their wagon of ice, delivering and selling to people who were fortunate enough to have an ice box so they could keep some cold items in the house, since there was no electricity for a refrigerator at that time. Or perhaps a family may have harvested and stored their own ice, if they had an ice box.

When we first moved in, I needed a washing machine and dryer but didn't really have any place to put it unless it would be in the kitchen. I later learned that Hilda Becker used to keep her ringer washer in the kitchen also. I bet she would have loved that addition of the laundry / entry room between the house and garage if Aaron would have had the opportunity to do it.

We found a Hoover portable washing machine on an auction. Since it was small, it seemed like the perfect fit for our home. I stored it beside the sink cabinet and would move it out in front of the sink when it was time to wash clothes. I attached the hoses to the water faucet and put the drain tube into the sink. Once I had the washer full and all the controls set, it was all automatic. It seemed like quite a step up from my mom's old ringer washing machine that I was familiar working with. With my mom's ringer washer, we had to fill the water in and set it to wash, and then run the clothes through the ringer to get the water out, instead of have a spin cycle to spin the water out. Then we put the drain hose down by the floor drain to drain the water out of the washer so we could fill it with clean water to wash the next load. In my little Hoover I could only wash 2 pair of jeans at a time. Rugs were very difficult for our little washer to get clean, so I often soaked them first in a pail of water. Other than rugs, it worked fine for the rest of our washing. Being the forgetful person that I am, there were a number of times that I forgot to put the drain tube into the sink. Then my kitchen floor got washed! I usually had to do some washing on the kitchen floor anyway after washing clothes because of all the spills around the sink. But the most interesting story of my forgetfulness with my Hoover was the day I was washing clothes when my sister, Dawn & her husband, Orville had arrived. I quickly went out to welcome them. Jim had seen them and come from the barn shortly thereafter. The four of us had a great visit and after a while had decided to come in the house. As I opened the screen door and could hear the water running, my memory suddenly returned. I had been filling the washing machine when they arrived but hadn't turned the water off! We now had at *least an inch of water all around the outside of the kitchen (the floor was higher in the middle so that part stayed dry). My floor got well washed that day. It really wasn't that much of a clean-up job though, because after turning the water off, it only took a few minutes and we realized the water was draining down through the floor. I didn't have to mop up any water. I just washed the floor. There was nothing water tight or air tight about this house.*

Shortly after we moved in, I was surprised to see a truck come driving up to the back door. On the side of the truck was printed, "Terrace Park Dairy". Ken Mathistad from Mt. Lake was the "milk man" and delivered milk and dairy products to homes in the area. This was not a new concept for me, but something we had never had at my parent's home. My dad milked dairy cows so I learned to know a different kind of milk truck. The "milk man" that came on my parent's yard was always a big, strong man who drove a large refrigerated truck with doors in the back that would swing open. He would drive up to our water tank where the milk cans were stored, and pull them up and into his truck. Then he would leave empty ones for dad to fill at the next milking. The idea of milk being delivered to my kitchen door was very appealing to me and I enjoyed the convenience of it.

We hadn't started out married life with much for material possessions. The money that my parents had helped me save for starting a college education had been used to fix up the house and purchase our living room and bedroom furniture. Jim had a car and this building site with a $10,000 mortgage, plus the $10,000 loan from his dad and another loan at the bank for the crop farming venture he had just begun on 80 acres. In those first weeks in our new home, we sat in the dining room and discussed our finances, the future of our farm and our dreams. These walls had surely heard other discussions during the past decades from previous occupants who were hoping and dreaming about what the future might hold for them. During the 1950's, the chicken barns had been built. It was most likely a step of faith to put them up and hope that they made enough of a return on the investment of the barns and *chickens to be able to pay for the barns and support the family with extra income. Our particular challenge was hoping that the price of feeder pigs would turn around soon so we could make loan payments and make improvements on the sow housing. I had to wonder how many families sat around the kitchen or dining room table in this house wondering if they could pay their bills and meet their financial commitments.*

Knowing our financial state of affairs, I realized it would be beneficial for me to have a job and bring in some extra income. After we settled into our home and I had put away the wedding presents and sent out the thank you notes, I went to Windom looking for a job. After one job interview, I started working four days a week as a waitress at Happy Chef Restaurant in Windom that first fall of our married life. This was the first time I ever had an interview for a job or worked steadily. Previously I had walked soybean fields for various farmers chopping or pulling out corn and cockleburs (before herbicides would take care of these weeds that limited yields). I also had a job in summer detasseling corn for the hybrid seed corn companies. These summer jobs all helped contribute to my college fund, which ended up being my home remodeling fund. As a waitress at Happy Chef I earned the minimum wage of $1.55 per hour but the dimes, quarters, and sometimes even dollars that I got for tips added up quickly and many times increased my take home pay by 50 to 100%. The tips were saved and used for items that were more of an extravagance than a need. We always kept my tips in a little brown money bag that advertised the Bingham Lake State Bank on the outside. Surely it wasn't gambling when Jim and I got out the money bag and played poker with my tips and returned them all to the bag at the end of the evening, was it? However, it may very well have been a first for this house to have poker played within its domain! I felt good that my wages were enough to buy groceries and any clothes that were necessary (we certainly couldn't afford anything that was a splurge).

When the tips bag had enough change in it, we were able to make the splurge to buy ourselves a color TV. Prior to that, we had a free small black and white TV that someone had given us. It was our first TV and sometimes we could even watch some news or programming on Channel 12 from Mankato if we had the "rabbit ears" (antenna) set right and the TV was cooperating with us. It had a mind of its own. It would go off whenever it pleased and then sometimes you couldn't get it to come back on. Wait a while and maybe it would work later. One night we both woke up to noise in the dining room and couldn't figure out in our drowsy state what was happening. As it turned out, the TV decided to turn on by itself during the middle of the night! Since there was no programming at night – it was just "white noise".

There was another night when we awoke to much scarier noises than the TV coming on by itself. One Saturday night within the first months of living in our house my parents had been over to visit, and Sandi had brought a bag packed to stay for night. Then when we would go to church on Sunday morning, she would go back home with my parents. We didn't have any spare beds yet, but

Sandi didn't mind sleeping on the sofa in the living room so that was her bed for night. I had gone to bed before Jim had come back in the house from checking the pigs in the farrowing barn, but hadn't fallen asleep until he was in bed with me. Suddenly, we were awakened to loud noises, like things were falling off the roof and hitting something metal down below. There was so much clanging and banging. Then we started to hear voices hollering. Jim pulled me close and said in a low voice, "I forgot to lock the back door when I came in from checking the barn". He quickly jumped out of bed and ran to the door with only his underwear on, but he was too late. They were already coming in. We were being "shivareed" by neighbors and the young people of the church. Gene and Margaret Duerksen (who had married just a few months before us) and Stan and Judy Rempel had helped organize a group of about 20 young people to come over after midnight with pots and pans and gather around our bedroom window and bang and clang and whoop and holler until they woke us up. Some of them (like Calvin Rempel and Allen Schroeder) thought it

*would be fun to walk in on us in the bedroom
and they got to the door before Jim had a
chance to lock it. But they were stopped in their
tracks as they entered through the kitchen door
and came into the dark dining room. They could
see, by the light of the yard light shining into
the living room, that there was someone
sleeping on the sofa. The thought was that we
weren't even sleeping together in the bedroom.
But someone found the lights and they soon
found out that it was Sandi sleeping on the
couch. At the same time, some of the girls my
age (Laverda Rempel, Elaine & Lavonne
Suderman, Nadine Friesen, etc) saw that Jim
was in the dining room too – dressed only in his
underwear. I think they were more embarrassed
than Jim! So he really made it a show, knowing
that his underwear had a hole in the back, he
put his hand under his underwear in the back
and poked his fingers out through the hole and
waved! Since Jim was already up, the guys
turned their attention to me and came walking
right in the bedroom. They threatened to pull
me out of bed if I didn't get up. Since I had
nothing on, I DID NOT want them to pull me out*

of bed. I promised to get up if they would let me get dressed first. So Jim closed the bedroom door and we both dressed quickly and got up. We came out in the dining room and I walked over to the sofa where Sandi was sitting with some of the girls and asked what she thought of all this. She was only 7 at the time and she said, "I thought it was a big drum". We looked around and said, "Well, we're up – now what?" Judy Rempel said, "Pancakes! Make us pancakes!" and the others chimed in with requests for breakfast items. So I made pancakes and we fed everyone and they left. A shivaree was not always done for young married couples, but it was done often enough that we had heard of it happening. I wonder if these walls had ever been through a shivaree before?

By fall, life had settled into a routine for us. The house felt like home, I had my job, and Jim had the pigs and helped his dad with the turkeys. It was time for Jim and his dad to work together harvesting the crops. They always filled the one small bin on our yard with the crops from the land Jim rented. Jim remembers very well one evening when he was hauling corn in to fill in that bin. His mother was along to help. I was already home from work, but since Jim was still working I took a nap. Since it was cold, I grabbed a blanket and lay down on the floor by the living room heater where it was nice and warm. If I heard activity on our yard, I would lift my head up and peek out the window to see if Jim was home for supper. As Jim & his mom came driving on the yard, I peeked out as usual. Jim wondered what his mom thought as my head would peek up into the window and then go back down. She never said anything or mentioned to either of us why it was she who was helping and not me.

We needed the corn and oats for the pigs, but the soybeans were a cash crop. Since my wages barely covered food and clothing, we needed the income from the pigs and soybeans to pay for gas, loan payments, and all the rest of the farm expenses. As we sat studying our farm record book and financial situation at the dining room table in mid 1973 (long before our financial records were computerized), we realized we were starting to make some progress with our financial situation. The price of feeder pigs was going up and we needed better facilities to house our growing sow herd. The sows were currently bedded down and housed in the shells of the old dairy barn and old chicken coup - with troughs outside for feeding in the morning and heated water tanks in winter for their drinking water. In winter it wasn't easy to get the snow out of the troughs and get feed into them before Jim got pushed around because the sows were hungry and wanted to eat RIGHT NOW; but it was nothing compared to a spring morning of rain and having to drag the troughs to higher ground and work in the mud and muck that sometimes ran into his shoes over the top of the five-buckle boots. Yes, he was dreaming of feeding pigs on cement! And wouldn't it be nice to have it close to the farrowing barn so there would be an alley to chase the sows through to bring them into the barn. Moving the sows across the yard, and into the farrowing barn was one of the farm jobs that I was recruited to help with. When I was not working at my job, I spent my time in the house or out on the yard, but very little time with the pigs or in the barn. The one job that I was really needed for, though, was to help create the illusion of a wall (using a piece of plywood) on one side of the sow while Jim did the same on the other side of the sow when we tried to walk them from the old barns to the farrowing barn. You see, we had no fences across the yard so Jim found it very helpful to have an extra person help him move sows. Sometimes they ended up running all the way back to the old dairy barn when we had them just up to the door of the farrowing barn. Other times they might get spooked and end up behind the house. Some of them just knew where to go and walked there nicely (with a little coaxing). Every now and then we had one that was wild and we tied ropes on her back legs so that if she took off running the wrong way, Jim could yank on the rope and pull her legs out from under her and slow her down. This is a trick he learned in Bolivia. He had watched Bolivian farmers walk pigs long distances with ropes tied on their back legs to keep them going the right direction. It was amazing how well it worked, but it was a hassle to tie ropes on their legs if they would walk across the yard and into the barn without any difficulties. Jim also dreamed of how nice it would be to have several different pens to keep the groups of sows separate. There was no possibility of having more than 2 groups of sows with the facilities we have now.

It would be a big step to put up new housing for 80 sows. Even though we both would have liked to have better housing for us, we realized the importance of keeping our livestock healthy and productive. This was the first time in our marriage that we were studying building plans and making our first changes to the yard. There would be many more changes to this yard that would come in the next few years.

Chapter 3

The old house walls that were now rapidly disintegrating in the flames had seen many changes both inside and outside. I looked at the empty spot where the tall old house had been setting. My mind flashed back through the decades – to the last time this spot on the yard sat clear and empty. I thought of the first farmer to have chosen this little hill in the middle of the quarter section to build a home for his family. The immigrants from Europe were all coming in during the early 1870's. The railroad had already received their allotment of land from the government and the rest of the plots in our area were ready to homestead. As an early settler would survey his new land to decide where the best place was to put his buildings, it's easy to see even today that the site where our buildings stand is the highest land in that quarter section. To the north of the building site, even in the 1950's when Jim remembers as a little boy, there was slough and pasture land. To the east, the land had already been tiled out by the 50's but it was obvious when it rained that the ground on that side of the farmstead must have been slough also. The land to the south of our building site was fairly level with the buildings, but to the west, there were several low spots and dips that would have drowned out in the early years of farming that land before tile was installed. It was important to keep the buildings on high ground, above the possibility of water running into them during spring thaw or heavy summer rains.

The image in my mind of a man standing on the hill where that old house stood and looking all directions may well have been an accurate historical account of how the buildings came to be placed on the parcel of land that has been home to us for almost 40 years. Peter Friesen was the first owner of this land as it was recorded in the abstract. He received a "homestead patent" on Feb. 13 of 1890 from the United States of America, by the President, Benjamin Harrison. This homestead was for the 80 acres which was the west ½ of the Northeast quarter of Section 14 in Carson Township. Necessity dictated that with the fierce Minnesota winters, shelter was needed for the animals as well as the people. It made *sense to build one building that would do both. The first building to be built on this yard was a house / barn combination, where the living quarters for people were on one side and the shelter for the animals was on the other. In the cold of winter, the heat from the animals helped to heat the house. A newspaper article from Nov. 18, 1875 describes how popular these types of buildings were in Carson township.*

"Mr. G. F. Robison, of Carson (township), tells us of the following new buildings in his township erected by the Mennonites: At the Kasaulkie place a barn 28 x 40, joined to a house 28 x 32. On C. Nixon's place a barn 18 x 42. On the Walch place a barn 24 x 27, joined to a house 18 x 24. On same quarter a house 18 x 40, joined to a barn 18 x 24. . . . ."

As we considered our new building plan to house our animals, it had similarities to the early settlers, in the fact that we were also contemplating when we would have new housing for us. I once told my mom that we couldn't put up a new house until we have a new barn for the sows to live in. It surprised her that we were even considering putting up a new house. My parents had never planned to build a new house but fate intervened and I was well aware of the story of how they got a new house when I was 8 years old:

When I was a young girl, we had lived in a small, one level, four room house that consisted of a kitchen/dining area, living room, and two small bedrooms (no bathroom). We lived on the same yard as my grandparents, who had a huge two story house. This was not the kind of two story farm homes that you may find on other area farms, where there was one or two bedrooms upstairs with slanted walls in the rooms as the slope of the roof came in. The five upstairs bedrooms in my Orloske grandparent's house were a full 7 feet, with an attic and roof above that. I often marveled at that big house when I was a child. When I would come up to the sidewalk to talk to grandma and grandpa, the house towered above me. While my parents never had any plans to build a new house, they were planning to add on to their little house in 1962. However, tragedy struck and my grandparent's big house burned to the ground. That December day of the fire changed many plans for both my grandparents and for my parents. The eventual outcome was that my parents moved into a new house that sat on almost the same spot where the big house burned down.

For now, any plans of a new house that we may have been cultivating in our minds were put on hold. Lying on the dining room table were the blueprints for a Cargill type open front structure of 10 attached hutches with a large cement frontage. The whole unit would take up a 70 by 110 foot space.

We were excited about this new barn. I wondered if the building plans for the dairy barn and the chicken coup had been as exciting to the inhabitants of this house years ago. Certainly, building the dairy barn was a big venture. It was hard for us to tell if it had been built after this house was built, but our suspicions were that it was. We knew from the abstract that Jacob T. Nickel purchased 160

*acres of land from Peter Friesen on Feb. 7, 1914
for $5600. We also knew from the 1926 plat
book of Carson Township that the same Jacob
T. Nickel (Pete Nickel's father and Aaron
Becker's father – in – law) was the owner of the
property at that time. Was he the one who built
the dairy barn and/ or the chicken coup? Were
his building plans all laid out on the table and
studied? It seemed a little ironic to be thinking
about how those two barns came to be built,
because as soon as we had new housing for our
hogs, it was our intention to demolish both of
those buildings.*

*Gradually over the first year and a half
of our marriage, I had begun to spend time in
the barns and helped along more and more
with the pigs. I remember the day in the winter
of 1973 that I was out in the chicken coup
looking at the sows and noticed one of them
that appeared to be "nesting" (getting ready to
have her pigs by digging a nest in the straw). As
I looked closer, she had quite an udder on her
and I thought she should be in the farrowing
barn. I went to the farrowing barn, where Jim
was working and told him that I thought we*

had missed one when we brought the last batch of sows in so he came to investigate. "Which one?" he asked, as he looked around. "She's right over there in the corner", I replied as I pointed out the sow. He jumped the fence and checked her. She was so close to having pigs that she already had milk. Even though it was almost dark, we quickly set up a crate in the barn and moved her in. Later that evening he came over and sat beside me on the sofa and put his arms around me. "I think God knew just the right woman to give me when I found you", he said quietly. I was a little surprised. It wasn't unusual for Jim to say he loved me but I had never heard that statement before. "Really, you think I'm the right one?" I teased.

"Today when you came and told me that you found a sow that needed to come in the barn, it really opened my eyes to the fact that we could be a pretty good team working with the pigs. Did you know you probably saved a whole litter of pigs?"

I actually was aware that if she had farrowed those pigs in that cold chicken coup, they never would have made it. Any that could have stayed close enough to her to warm up and dry off would surely have been laid on at some point. We were both beginning to realize that if I stayed home and worked in the barn, I could help bring in more farm income with better productivity. I was also aware of the fact that I was the first of a new generation living in this house to be working outside of the home. I was quite sure that all the other homemakers who had lived within these walls may have been busy working in the house and on the farm, but most likely never received a paycheck from a business outside the farm.

Farm wives had their ways of earning cash for special gifts, clothes, or events. One of the most common was to retain the income from the sale of eggs. Some farm wives of earlier generations took care of the chicken feeding and gathering of eggs, cleaned and packed the eggs, and took them to town (perhaps with the help of sons or husbands to lift the heavy egg cases for them). The money they were paid at the store for the eggs was either grocery money or cash saved for special occasions. This household was no different. I knew that Mrs. Aaron Becker sold eggs to the neighbors, because Jim would bicycle over to this yard as a youngster to purchase eggs for his mother. It may well have been a special fund for her, but it also served to provide the community families with eggs if they didn't happen to have chickens. Did these walls hold secrets of special jars and secret hiding places for money that the children wouldn't find or know about?

Chapter 4

How many secrets were burning up with these walls as they slowly turned from wood to ashes? Did they remain secrets or were they found out long before the secret was to be revealed like my secret?

I had the brilliant idea that it would be special to make a gift for Jim for Christmas. What could I make? I knew how to knit some basic stitches. Maybe I could make a sweater. I searched for patterns and found one for a vest – perfect! I shopped for yarn and choose a verigated dark purple, fushia, and black yarn and the correct size needles that the pattern called for. I was on my way. I began my project whenever I was in the house doing household chores and Jim was in the barn. I would begin making a meal and go to the bedroom and work on the project, run back to the kitchen and check on the meal, and head back to the bedroom, etc. It took a lot of time to run back and forth but I couldn't take the chance that Jim would come walking in the door. If I was working on the project in the bedroom and he would come in the door, I quickly put it away and left the room. I found that I didn't really have that much time alone in the house so I began getting braver and would work on it while he was reading or watching TV. I would sit on the bed facing away from the door so that if I heard him come walking to the bedroom, I could quickly slip my project under the covers or the bed. I was almost done with the front side, but I still had the back to make and then put it together. Christmas was coming fast and I couldn't see how I would get it done at this rate. I began taking more and more chances and thinking that Jim was pretty dense not to have caught on to the fact that I had a secret. He almost caught me several times and once he even asked what I was doing in the bedroom. I came up with some lame excuse and he accepted it. One noon meal, when I thought I had dodged another close call, we sat down at the table for our meal. Jim said, "Let's pray" and bowed his head. As I bowed my head and closed my eyes, I heard him get up. I looked up and he was running to the bedroom. I ran after him calling, "No, no, don't go in there" afraid that he would pull back the covers and reveal the gift before I had a chance to hide it. He just laughed and asked, "Why not?" "Because it's a secret" I replied. It was left at that until that evening. I knew I had to be able to work on it in front of him if I was to get it done so I brought out the unfinished sweater and told him all about it and that if I was going to be able to give it to him for Christmas I had to be able to work on it a lot more. It was the end of my secret but Jim was proud of that sweater and wore it often. Years later I finally told him he didn't need to wear that sweater anymore just to make me feel good, but he said he liked it. Secret or not, it had been worth it.

Christmas in the old house, taken from the dining room table looking into the living room.

By the spring of 1974, I had decided to quit working at Happy Chef and stay home to help with the farming. We found it interesting and funny that there were many whispers and wonderings if I was pregnant because I quit my job. Surely I was now going to stay home and raise babies. We first heard about it from Jim's mother. We were keenly aware that when she was telling us that some of the ladies at church were wondering if we were expecting a baby, that she was also hunting for clues as to whether this was true.

The open front in the winter of 1975

The new open front building went up in the summer of 1974. We had made a lot of progress in paying off our loans and were able to get a loan for $14,000 for our new barn. The landscape of the yard changed quickly after that. We no longer needed the big old dairy barn or the low, long chicken barn. Over the next few years both of these buildings were razed. Jim's brother, Ron, used lumber from the old dairy barn to build a new garage on his yard in North Mankato. As a thank you for the lumber, they helped us tear down the barn. Once these buildings were gone, the circular effect of the farm buildings encircling the yard light pole disappeared. Our house seemed to stand alone on the hill, as if to say in defiance, "The other old buildings may be gone, but I will not be moved".

We felt very blessed that our farming venture was going well enough to make an improvement like this. We wanted to celebrate our accomplishment and at the same time share with our neighbors and church family some of the wonderful pork we produced. It was a relatively new idea in our community, but we had heard of people who had roasters large enough to rotisserie a whole hog. We chose a date and invited neighbors, friends, and the church for a whole hog roast. They could bring a salad or dessert and we furnished all the meat. We were beginning a celebration tradition that was repeated many times and for various reasons throughout our marriage. The preparations were exciting and fun. We took the pig to the butcher shop, rented the roaster, got the back yard all spiffed up, and set up a butchering table on sawhorses to cut up the meat when the pig was cooked. The morning of the roast, we made an early trip to town with the pickup and brought the butchered hog home, wrapped it in chicken wire, got the fire going, and placed the pig on the spit. We watched it all day but also had other things to get ready so we weren't in front of it the whole time. We were quite surprised to come back to the roaster one time and find the flames about 10 feet high. Our pig was now all charred. Would it be okay? We couldn't back out now. We hoped there would be plenty of good meat on the inside. After 8 hours of roasting, it certainly appeared that the hog was done, as it was starting to fall apart.

Jim roasting a hog

People were starting to arrive. Jim was pleased to show the open front to any of the men who were interested. In between visiting, I was trying to get the koolaid and coffee ready. I took a few minutes to change clothes and hurried back out to the back yard with the koolaid. About half of our guests were here. My mom came over to me quickly and pulled me aside, "Diane, I can't believe you would invite the church and then wear an outfit that shows your tummy button!" Jim was still changing clothes in the bedroom so I went in to see what he thought about my outfit. I had just thrown on something comfortable because it was a hot day. The style at that time was short tops that would come not quite to the waist. I happened to pick a pair of shorts with a lower waist line so that it was just barely below my waist, so yes, it was true: you could see inches of my middrift, sometimes including my tummy button. He said, "You look fine, what's the big deal with your tummy button showing?" So it was decided – my husband had more input in my clothing choices than my mother! All in all, it was an enjoyable evening and we heard many compliments on the meat. It turned out that the charred outside kept the moisture in and made the meat delicious. People expressed their appreciation and many stood around and picked at the bones, nibbling on the meat until after dark.

We had other parties and good times of fellowship while we lived in that house. Our families would come to visit. We had friends over for lunch or meals. These walls were familiar with the sounds of family and friends enjoying each other's company. The Nickel families that lived here before us had happy family gathering times also. Lori Krause told me of the enjoyment of remembering happy family gatherings when she would go to visit her cousins at "Uncle Aaron's house". The children would play upstairs and hear, through the open grate, the sounds of the adults visiting downstairs in the living room. In July, they would enjoy picking mulberries from the big mulberry tree north of the house. I can imagine these children coming back in with purple hands, and possibly feet, if they were barefoot.

Jim's 65 Chevy had done well for us, but had a lot of miles, and I always hated that added air conditioner unit that didn't leave room for my legs if I sat close to him. Even though we were already married, I still sat in the middle of the front bench seat, as I had done while we were dating. As we were driving through Mankato one day, Jim pointed to the car dealership and said, "Look at that". It was a blue Roadrunner with white pinstripes. He turned our 65 Chevy around and said, "I have to go see it". It was a new 73 model, but this was already summer of 74 and they were anxious to move this car. After a test drive and some dealing, we drove home in a new car! We paid $4,000 and my husband had the car of this dreams. What a sharp looking car to sit in front of this ordinary house. I could easily feature a model A or maybe a Chevy or Dodge from the 40s or 50s sitting by the sidewalk, but a Roadrunner really jazzed the place up!

Harvest was done early in the fall of 1974 and we had ideas of how to use the nice fall weather. In the past, Jim had gone up to the boundary waters on fishing trips in spring with his brother, Ron, and friends. I had wanted to go along, but quickly found out it was a "men only" trip. Jim had always wondered if fishing was good in fall too. Now we had a chance to find out. We quickly made plans for a 3- or 4 - day fishing trip during the first week of November. Apparently, we hadn't lived through enough early November snowstorms yet to have the thought cross our minds that we could get caught in a storm. We packed our new

Roadrunner with a tent, LP gas tank & heater, sleeping bags, food, a boat motor, and fishing equipment. We thought we were well prepared as we headed up to Duluth and then up the Gunflint trail. We had been in this area and stayed in a cabin on our honeymoon in August but at this time of the year everything looked so deserted. We had a hard time finding any outfitters open, but finally found someone who was willing to rent us a boat. They gave us a map with the campsites listed. They were quite curious that we wanted to go fishing now. That should have been a clue to us. Out on the lake it was quiet and foggy – about 50 degrees. The lake was very eerie with the quietness, fog, and the call of loons. We felt very alone but didn't really mind. It was beautiful and we were sure there would be good fishing. We spent a lot of time out fishing over the next two days but didn't even get a nibble. It was enjoyable to spend time together in a different setting than the barns. We expected to have seen some other people but there was no hint that anyone else was on the lake except for once when we thought we heard a distant motor. We hadn't needed the heater yet. Cuddling together in our zipped together sleeping bags had been warm enough, but the third night the temperature was falling. As we left the campfire that night, it had started to rain and the wind was strong. We started the heater and slept fairly well, but we were both well aware that the rain and wind were pounding against the side of the tent. The heater couldn't keep up with the cold wind, but we had to stay until daylight and neither of us was interested in venturing out of our cozy nest. The sleeping bags were getting wet from the water running in and we couldn't stay dry or warm any longer. Fortunately, it was now daylight. We dressed as warm as we could and discovered that the rain had turned to snow. We were in the middle of a snowstorm! After two days of glass like still waters, today's waters were total whitecaps pounding at the shoreline. How would we get back across the lake? We would have to take a much longer route along the shoreline and then make a dash across an open part of the lake to get back to our car. It would be a challenging trip. I could tell from the look on Jim's face as we packed everything back in our boat that he was contemplating if we could make it back through these waves. We both knew that we had no choice. We couldn't stay – the weather would only get worse. We simply had to make it back. We started out along the shore line, as close as we dare stay with the way the waves were throwing our boat around. The water was splashing up on us, and the sleet and snow was hitting us in the face. We were already getting wet under our rain jackets. Even though the progress was slow, we could see we were getting closer to the main part of the lake. Soon it would be time to head out across the open part of the lake. We were headed into the wind. I turned my head so the sleet didn't hit my face, but Jim didn't have that luxury. He had to keep our boat on track to find the right island to head along the shoreline and find our way back to the car. Our boat was rocking up and over the waves, but we were hitting them head on instead of the more dangerous possibility of having them hit our boat sideways and rock it from side to side, perhaps flipping it over. Hitting the waves head on had a lot of disadvantages, though, when the spray of water kept coming up and over the front of the boat. We were both soaked and so cold by the time we made it back to shore. Jim went immediately and started the car. I had always tried to be a trooper and help out, but I couldn't move anymore. I simply had to warm up in the car for a while. A new worry was on Jim's mind as he saw all the snow piling up on the gravel road and he wasn't willing to take time to warm up. He knew we needed to get out of here as soon as possible. I helped unload the last few items, even though I wasn't fully warm yet. We had a chance to warm up in the car, and then headed out on the backwoods road that had some construction just up the road. The construction area was tough to get through and we got stuck a number of times and then managed to get moving again. Once we were stuck so badly we couldn't move anymore. A payloader was working on the road and, as he went by, he noticed we were really stuck. He came over and gave us a push and we were back on our way. It was such a relief to get to the fork in the road that put us on a better *road. We breathed a sigh of relief once we were back on a paved road and headed south along the north shore drive by Lake Superior. We stopped at Grand Marais and watched the waves rolling up and over the sea wall. We got the bright idea to park the car by the wall and got a free car wash, which was desperately needed after those muddy roads. When we got back home and told my parents the story of our adventure they commented that we better not do anything that foolish after we have children! It occurred to us that it could have been a sad time for our families to take care of our belongings in the house if we had drowned in the storm that day.*

There already had been sad times in this house as a loved one was mourned. Both Jacob & Maria Nickel had passed away while they had been living in this house. In fact, we had heard that Maria's coffin and viewing were actually held within the house. Jim also remembered the time when his neighbor, Hilda Becker passed away during the time that she and Aaron lived in this house. Pete Nickels had also lost a daughter who was only 10 years old.

These walls had been through many tears and times of grieving, even though that had not been an experience of ours during the time we lived there.

Chapter 5

The hot blaze in front of me brought to mind how good this would feel during a cold blizzard. This old house had weathered many storms, but the most notable for us was the Super Bowl Blizzard of 1975. We were always up for an adventure and as this storm came blowing in, it certainly was an adventure. We were already very familiar with how the heating system in our house worked (or many times didn't work!) We didn't have a central heating system in our house at the time we moved into it, although we could see that at some point there had been some kind of central heater in a corner of the living room, which would have been almost in the center of the house. Perhaps it was an oil burning heater, which I was familiar with from the little house I lived in until I was 8. Many evenings and even days were spent lying on the floor with a blanket in front of that heater that blew warm air out of the vents in the bottom, by the floor. Perhaps the heater in this house was a wood burning stove. We didn't know what kind of stove it was or the fuel it used, but we did know that there was a chimney in the small bedroom upstairs and a grate in the floor in the large upstairs bedroom that was located directly above the living room. The opening in the ceiling of the living room had been covered and papered before we moved in so the warm air couldn't escape to the upstairs bedroom any more, but relatives still remember the stove in the living room and the heat coming up through the grate in the bedroom upstairs.

The heating system that we used in the house had been put in by Aaron Becker and probably worked well when it was new. Each room – bedroom, dining room, living room and kitchen – had its own individual LP gas heater that was vented to the outside and ran along the baseboard about 8 feet long and a foot high. They each had a pilot light and temperature control. When the flame was lit and called for heat, the flame heated a heat exchanger. The problem was that the heat exchangers had cracked over time so they were no longer tight, which allowed air movement through the heat exchanger and, in turn, would blow out the pilot light in windy weather. The kitchen had an upright unit stationed by the outside door, but the heat exchanger on that unit had never cracked. We had already learned during the first winter in our house how easily our bedroom heater blew out overnight if there was any wind at all, and needed to be relit in the morning. It didn't help that it was on the northwest corner of the house and that's where the winter winds came from. The living room heater often blew out, too, but we could always count on the kitchen heater to work. Most of the time, the dining room heater stayed on also.

We already had snow on the ground by the time January rolled around in 1975. The snow started anew on Friday, along with a strong wind. After hearing the weather forecast, we prepared for the storm by moving the mattress from our bed into the living room on Friday. This ordeal of moving the mattress had become common practice whenever there was wind and cold weather because our bedroom heater was becoming less dependable every winter and it didn't take long for the temperature in the bedroom to get below 60 degrees. We had bedded the pigs in our new open front building in the morning hoping to make it through the storm. By evening the lights were flickering and we wondered how long we would have electricity. We awoke Saturday morning to a cold house and no electricity. We only had the kitchen heater left going and although Jim tried to light the heater in the dining room, it wouldn't keep going long enough to get any heat out of it before it blew out again. We couldn't spend too much time on the heater because the pigs had to be checked to see how they were doing without electricity. We bundled up in layers of clothes with ski masks and scarves so that only our eyes were subjected to the snow and wind. There was so much snow on the living room window that we could hardly see out. Snow tends to stick to the windows in a bad storm.

The dining room window had less snow on it, but we could hardly believe that the tree that stood only 10 feet from the house was so hard to see sometimes. We had usually gauged a bad blizzard by a wind so strong that it was difficult to make out the grove that stood 500

After the storm: a picture of the front of the house taken from the yard light pole.

feet behind that tree and the house; or if we looked out to the front yard, low visibility of the granary / machine shed that was about the same distance away in the front of the house. Now we couldn't see anything in front of the house, not even the yard light pole.

We opened the kitchen door to the inside, but there was so much snow in front of the screen door to push away we couldn't get it open. It was time to check the front door. We could get out the front door, but making our way to the barn was a challenge. We followed the house to the garage and then had to head off to the south east, not being able to see anything except each other at times. It was a struggle to keep our eyes open in the blowing snow and it was very hard to judge how deep the snow was because it was moving so much below my waist. We knew our yard well and knew where each tree was so we made it from tree to tree, sometimes wading through thigh deep snow banks and sometimes walking on top of them.

When we made it to the barn it felt so good to wipe all the cold frozen snow off our eyelashes and take the scarves off. Maybe a person would be able to see better if there weren't so much snow blowing in your eyes. But then we remembered how it had looked when we looked out the window and we thought we did well to see as much as we did on our way to the barn. The sows in the farrowing barn needed water to produce milk for the baby pigs, but without electricity, we had no pump running to pressure the water lines. We brought in snow and gave each sow a feeder full of snow that would soon melt in this warm barn that gained extra heat from little LP heaters hung between the crates to keep the baby pigs warm. We weren't too concerned about the barn fans not running because the wind was so strong, there was a certain amount of air moving in the barn without the fans.

Our next problem was the sows on the open front needing more bedding with all the snow blowing in on them. It was no surprise to see their backs all white with snow and the bedding was pretty wet. We had no toboggan to pull the bales over the snow drifts and we could never carry them through this deep snow and blizzard. We had a dilemma on our hands. How could we get the bedding to the sows to keep them warm, instead of letting them get wet and cold? Suddenly, as we were standing in one of the hutches, an idea came to us both that the hood from an old junked out car could *be our toboggan. It was already taken off and just needed a rope so we could both pull it. It worked great, but we felt like a couple of oxen hitched up to a yoke! We pulled 6 bales at a time. They were loaded from the old chicken barn, pulled around the farrowing barn, and up and on top of the roof of the open front since the snow had piled all the way to the back roof line. From the roof, we could just toss them down and into the hutches.*

After finishing the hours of chores, we spent the rest of the day sitting in our kitchen in front of the heater, playing cards and games and occasionally listening to the battery operated radio. We didn't want to run the batteries down too much so we were careful how much we listened. It was a challenge to find something to eat that didn't need our electric stove to cook it. Even if there had been microwave ovens at this time, it wouldn't have helped because they need electricity too. It would be almost a decade before we actually owned a microwave. The refrigerator was no problem in a cold house that was getting colder all the time.

That night we moved the mattress into the kitchen and piled on all the blankets I could find. We were camping in a blizzard – wasn't this fun?? Those were the days we enjoyed an adventure since it was just the two of us, we were young and strong and enjoyed the challenge. However, we were hoping the storm would be over soon because a cold house and cold food gets old in a hurry. Besides that, we wanted to watch the Vikings play on TV in the Super Bowl on Sunday. We checked the temperature in the morning – 45 degrees in the kitchen, the warmest room in the house. The bedroom was probably close to freezing. We began to worry that the pipes in the bathroom might freeze, but we had the faucets open to allow some room for expansion and thanks to the bales around the foundation and the extra snow, the pipes under the house were well insulated.

Sunday morning brought little relief but the visibility was somewhat better. With the electricity still off, we had basically the same chores to do again in the morning. We made sure we were done with the chores in time to *listen to the Super Bowl on the radio. If we ran low on battery power while listening to the game, so be it. What a disappointment that after using all that battery power the Vikings lost another one! We later heard stories of how others had fared during the blizzard and power outage and realized our one lone surviving heater had done well to keep our house above freezing. Many homes froze and had broken water pipes. One story we heard was from my cousin's family of 4 who put blankets and pillows under their table and draped the table with blankets. They made this makeshift teepee their home for 2 days as they tried to make one warm spot in a freezing house.*

After the storm, a picture of the house and garage from the north

Chapter 6

We were making new stories to be told to future generations. This old, ordinary house already abounded with a rich history of stories that were heard within these walls. From the time this house was built, there very well may have been stories told of foreign lands across the sea. The first inhabitants - either Peter Friesens, or Jacob Nickels were more than likely either born in Europe or had parents who had been born there. I pondered the tales that may have been told of the trip over the ocean and then the adventure in this new land with a strange language, as they traveled by rail to fulfill hopes and dreams for the future. I knew that during the life of this house there were plans made for other travels to distant U.S. states, like Alaska, and most likely stories told as they returned to visit family members who lived within these walls. Pete Nickel had lived here before he went to Alaska, and the following inhabitants, Aaron Beckers, were family members, who probably heard those stories.

When we moved into the house, the stories of foreign lands were not stories from Europe or Alaska, but stories from South America. I had heard some of the stories as we were dating before we were married, but many more stories came out as we shared our past with each other within the confines of this dwelling. It had only been a few years since Jim had returned from Bolivia when we moved into the house. I was fascinated with hearing of the people he had come in contact with, and adventures he had in Bolivia. It wasn't long before he started to tell me that we would take a trip to Bolivia together. He wanted me to be able to share a land and people that he had come to love. We began to make plans for this trip. It had to be planned when there were no sows farrowing, so four months in advance we had the boars in their separate pens to make sure we had no surprise litters while we were gone. The itinerary was for us to fly to Peru and stay there for a few days, then on to Cochabamba and Santa Cruz, Bolivia. We would have 12 days in Bolivia before spending the last couple days in Rio De Janeiro, Brazil, then head *back home. There was much excitement and anticipation in making these travel preparations. Even though I had traveled to the West Coast through all the northwestern tier of states, and Colorado & Wisconsin on family vacations with my parents and family, I had never yet stepped on soil that wasn't a part of the United States. It was thrilling to think of traveling to these South American countries. The winter had been hard and taken its toll on Jim's disposition. He spent many long days cleaning off the open front so he could feed the sows. In the cold, it took a lot of his time to thaw water fountains. I was looking forward to the break from winter and hoping I would see a more cheerful husband in a warmer climate.*

Jim had spent much time helping his dad gather turkey eggs and inseminating and loading turkeys over the years. It was only natural to ask dad to do the chores while we were gone. With preparations for chores made, vaccinations finished, passports and luggage in hand, we were off to Bolivia in February of 1975. I was sick most of the time in Peru, but the city of Lima gave me my first glimpse of third world culture. This was Jim's first time in Peru also. We were in awe at seeing government buildings with bullet holes in them and soldiers standing around with their machine guns in hand, after the recent unrest. I never imagined there might be corners of city streets that were used as public bathrooms! I was the most sick the day we arrived in Bolivia. I had a high fever, but it broke shortly after we got off the plane so I was able to travel to the hotel in Cochabamba where we stayed for a few days. We walked around the city that he had called home when he first came to Bolivia. This was the place he had stayed while he was in language school. There were many stories of adventures had by these young men, who were learning a foreign culture and language for the first time. It was a beautiful city, set in the mountains, and I enjoyed the time there, but it was soon time to move on. Our next stop was Santa Cruz, then Montero. We met many of Jim's friends and coworkers. It had only been 6 years since he left but already there were some changes. We spent most of our time at the school in Montero, where we stayed in the room he had lived in when he taught there. It was no longer a vocational school so the hog set up he had improved was now under brush. I certainly had a much better understanding of the stories and conditions that he lived in. We decided to take a trip out to Yappacanee to visit a friend of Jim's that grew up in the U.S., married a girl from Germany, and was now trying to make it farming in Bolivia. After a long trip, we arrived late in the day. He wasn't home, but his wife greeted us and introduced us to their 2- year old daughter and 2- day old baby! We didn't want to impose, but she knew as well as we did, that we probably could not find transportation to make it back that evening so we were invited to stay for night. Jim's friend arrived during the night. After visiting in the morning, he took us to meet the bus. We had many other interesting experiences and visits in Bolivia. Too quickly it was time to leave Bolivia and fly to Rio de Janeiro in Brazil to unwind and relax by the ocean. The days in Rio were quite a contrast to our time in Bolivia. We were suddenly only tourists, no longer treated as friends or guests. However, our accommodations were wonderful, and we loved the time on the beach. After 2 days in Brazil, we were ready to head back to winter in Minnesota. We had spent a couple weeks in the heat of summer in South America. Jim's disposition was back to normal, and I was beginning to think of new plans for our future.

Chapter 7

I watched little Juli running around by the fire. Was she old enough to remember this ordinary old house that was her first home? As I watched her, I thought of those first desires to begin a family. When we married, we both were happy to make sure there was a space of time for just the two of us. We didn't know when we might want a family, but we knew it wasn't right away. Slowly, over the first three years, I was beginning to think about little ones in our house. I was imagining years ago as little feet came bounding down the steps on a cold morning to stand by the heater in the center of the living room and warm up. Back in the 1920s, Jacob and Maria Nickel were raising a family of 5 girls and two boys. I could imagine how busy and active that household must have been. It must have been so nice for those children to only have to walk ½ mile to the country school house at the corner. I could imagine the noise level with all seven children gathered around the table. The next generation to live here were Pete and Alvina Nickel. During the earlier years of their marriage, Pete's two youngest siblings (Hilda and Ben) were living here with them, since Jacob and Maria had died before their youngest children were adults. Later, as Pete and Alvina had four daughters of their own, I could imagine the dolls occupying the bedrooms and dresses in the closets. I was also imagining the busy activities of two boys while Aaron Beckers lived here during the 1940s. How many children had laughed and cried in this house, within the life of these walls?

One day I asked Jim, "Do you think it's time for us to start a family?" "I'm happy the way things are", he responded. Maybe I was too. It was dropped. Something just seemed missing. Did I really love children? Would I make a good mother? Could I teach them what they needed to live happy, healthy, lives in tune with God? I questioned these things. I was never much of a baby lover and I wondered what it would be like to have my own baby. I looked forward to the toddler days and imagined exploring the house and yard with a little one as *they were learning to talk. Time had passed as I pondered these things. I had come to some conclusions and brought up the subject again. "I think I want to have a baby." This time I would find out how he felt about my desires instead of just a general concept. "Is that what you really want?" I affirmed again that I had decided I was ready. His response was, "Well then, let's have a baby." With that, the birth control was eliminated and I anxiously waited to find out if I was pregnant. Life went on and the months passed by . . . .*

Another harvest was upon us. After I had quit my job, I had begun riding along with Jim as he hauled loads of soybeans and corn home during harvest. Sometimes I stayed home and worked with the pigs, but many days I was free to spend with my husband, and he enjoyed the company. His father was the combine operator and Jim took care of hauling the loads, unloading, and drying corn. I learned how to watch the batch corn dryer and sometimes stayed on the yard to turn it off at the right time.

At first, as I started working more with Jim and his dad, we all had lunch and even ate meals together at his mom and dad's house. Jim's mom, Viola, was very gracious to make all the food, which she loved doing, and either sent it with us to the field (afternoon lunch) or we would wash up and come in and eat (noon or evening meal). I was still too young to understand that I shouldn't be taking advantage of her generosity so much. This particular fall, Viola's uncle Albert Flaming was coming for a visit. I knew she was working hard to make it special for him. I was under the impression that he wanted to get in on the harvest, but Jim's mom would have found it much easier if they could have dropped everything and just entertained him. Albert's sister, Hulda, (Jim's grandmother), was in the Good Samaritan nursing home in Mountain Lake at the time, so Viola spent time there visiting with her mother and Albert. This left her very little time to make the kind of very special meals that she wanted to make for his visit. And then there was the dilemma of Jim & myself always just assuming it would be okay to eat at their home. One night as we were coming in to wash up, Jim's mother asked me what we were having for supper. I answered that I had been in the field with Jim all day and I didn't have any supper ready. She said, "Oh. Well, then I'll put plates on the table for you". I could tell by the tone of her response that we should have been eating at home. After that, we rarely ate meals at their home without being invited first, but we were often invited. We never felt bad about accepting the afternoon lunches, however. Mom was too good of a cook to refuse any of her goodies!

As harvest was finishing up I was beginning to wonder if it could possibly be. Could I be pregnant? We had waited many months, but now we had to spend these days of limbo wondering if it was really true. You see, there were no pregnancy tests that could be purchased at the drug store at that time. After a few weeks, I called the clinic. I was told I should really be about 2 months along before the doctor examines me. Early in December I was in to see Dr. Wiens, and it was confirmed that we would have a baby in July. What excitement that news brought into this old house! How many different ways had previous families celebrated the news of a new little one joining the family? Did the rooms get remodeled to include a special room for the baby? We really didn't have much choice as to where the baby would be sleeping. If it was not in our room, it would have to be in the dining room or living room because we didn't use the 2nd story of the house.

We planned to tell our families at the family Christmas celebration we had with each of our respective families. It was hard to wait and keep this secret, but the time finally came. When we told the news to my family, the most excitement came from Sandi (11) and Sue (16). They were ready to be aunts and looked forward to babysitting and having a new baby in the family. This would be the first grandchild for my parents and my mom still had her two youngest children at home. Even if the idea of being grandma appealed to her, she knew she couldn't devote a lot of time to it for quite a few years. As it turned out, she may not have spent as much time with my children as she wished, but she may have spent more time with my grandchildren (her great grandchildren) than I did. Since she was a young grandma, her great grandchildren were the ones who received a lot of attention from her when they were little. All in all, our exciting baby news was very happily received in my family.

It was time to tell the news to Jim's family who had gathered at his parent's house. Since Jim had 2 older brothers who were married and had children who were the same age as my youngest sister, the house was full of activity. Our news was greeted with much enthusiasm. Jim's mom was pleased that all the work she just spent that fall repainting the playhouse would now have even more purpose. The older grandchildren still enjoyed playing in the cute little 6 x 8 foot playhouse in the backyard, but they were growing out of it. Our baby would be the 6th grandchild on this side of the family. Jim's brothers and their wives were excited for us, as was his younger sister. But nothing matched the excitement of the nieces and nephews. They hadn't said much when we made our announcement. It wasn't until later, as they all came bouncing down the stairs, bubbling with enthusiasm over their new found activity that we all realized what entertainment this news had given them. The first time down the stairs, they had a list of names for our baby – from A to Z. The next time they came giggling down the steps, we were given a listing of names for twins and triplets. After reading off these names and getting the appropriate laughter from the adults that they had desired, they took off again, running up the stairs with their next challenge, carrying the noise and laughter with them. This was keeping them occupied for hours, and we could hear the howling laughter that it was creating upstairs. They had laughed so much, they could hardly talk the next time they came bounding back down the stairs. Kevin was appointed spokesperson, because he wasn't giggling as much as the girls, but even he had a hard time making it through the next reading of names without laughter. We now had a list of names, not only for twins or triplets, but for quadruplets, quintuplets, and sextuplets! The lists got sillier as they went, but we all enjoyed the good laughter.

I didn't have much of a sewing machine until Jim bought me a new Bernina. I had even taken some classes to learn how to use all the features it had. During the winter would be a good time to start doing some sewing for my baby. My excitement was building as I made clothes for this new baby. These walls never told their secrets, but I was sure that there had been other mothers-to-be that had busily worked on preparing clothes and blankets for a new baby.

Valentine's Day brought a special gift from Jim. His excitement was growing too. My gift this Valentine's Day was a record. Our house had heard a lot of music played during these past four years. Jim had a stereo system with speakers that had a turntable to play records. Our house never did live long enough to hear music from CDs or ipods, but we still had music. The first vinyl records that came out were about 8" in diameter and called 78s, because you played them at a speed of 78 *revolutions per minute. By the time I was a child, there were 2 more speeds and sizes. The children's records that I had were mostly 45s and a little smaller (about 6" in diameter) than the 78s. The majority of the records we used were albums that were about 10" in diameter that ran at a speed of 33. When I was a little girl, it was so much fun to put records on the turntable at the wrong speed and listen to the people singing so fast and high, they sounded like "the chipmunks" or put it on 33 and listen to a deep bass voice that sang so slow. Jim and I had many of the records that were put out by "the Carpenters", a brother and sister singing group that we loved to listen to. We had many other records from popular music groups from the 60s and 70s, like the Beachboys, Herb Albert & the Tijuana Brass, etc. A song that had hit the pop charts over the past year was named "Havin' my Baby". The record Jim bought for me had that song on it, along with other love songs. Some of the words in the song were:* "Havin' my baby – what a lovely way to say how much you love me". *It was a special song for us all through the pregnancy.*

That winter we got a letter from Jim Nightengale, asking if he could come and work on our farm because he had always wanted to be a farmer. His parents were missionaries in Brazil, but had formerly had a pastorate in Mountain Lake, which is why Jim was interested in coming back to Mt. Lake. We accepted his offer, but told him we couldn't pay him much because we really didn't need any hired help. I was thinking that this year it might be nice to have someone who could help with rock picking since I was pregnant. Jim N. arrived while my husband was gone on a fishing trip to the boundary waters (yes, he tried it again!). We had set up a bedroom upstairs so Jim N. settled in, and I gave him a tour of the farm. No one had stayed in that north room for at least a decade. He helped with the pigs, but we could tell he was not a hog farmer. Many little things slipped right by him. He helped pick rocks but became bored with that. Perhaps he had hopes of running more important equipment. One night he invited his high school friend, Randy Ewert, over. I had made supper for them and the guys retired to Jim's upstairs room. They were making noise and carrying on. We wondered what they were doing up there! Later we realized that what sounded like jumping on the bed – had really been jumping on the bed. The bed was quite broken but not a word was mentioned by Jim or by us. I was trying to imagine what it looked like for two college age boys to jump on a bed. My guess is that it wasn't the first bed jumping that was done in that room. I thought of Aaron Becker's boys, or Jacob Nickel's boys (Pete and Ben) who may well have had their beds in that room. Could they have jumped on beds? If these college boys did it, it wouldn't be any surprise if younger boys did also. Jim N. stayed about a month and then suddenly left to stay at Maranatha Ministries in Delft, while he meditated on his future. Years later, he was a missionary in Brazil, to which he was much more suited than farming. Jim Nightengale was the first of many guests who made their home with us for weeks or months.

Our new crop of corn and soybeans was up and growing. It was always important to walk through the soybean fields and remove the unwanted corn and weeds. We used the chemical, treflan, that kept the grasses down but at that time, there was nothing that could be sprayed to take care of the broadleaf weeds, so most farmers walked through their fields with hoes, corn knives, or even bare hands, chopping or pulling corn and weeds. Usually the weeds of concern were cockelburrs, lambsquarter, mustard, and thistles. We had very little trouble with anything other than cockelburrs, but we wanted the corn out too. Jim's dad had made knives to cut the weeds by using a 4 to 5 foot piece of pipe with a triangle knife from the soybean head cutting bar of the combine welded at the end of it. These were like a poker. The pipe was the handle and you poked at the weed or the corn plants and the sharp knife at the end would cut it right off. With all the walking through soybean fields I had done during my teen years, I had never seen anyone use a tool that worked so well to remove the weeds. We often worked in the fields together with Jim's dad and many times his mom would join us. One year on a July day we were walking the bean fields on a farm a *few miles south of Jim's parents place. His mom had the idea that we should have a picnic. We both contributed some food and brought along a blanket to sit on for our picnic. It turned out to be a cold day. When we stopped at noon, we draped the blanket over our shoulders instead of sitting on it and had a very cold picnic.*

The year I was pregnant, we were walking the fields on the home farm during the first week of July. Each person would walk between the middle of the four rows and watch those rows for corn and weeds. Jim and I usually walked together, but Jim's mom had a hard time keeping up with our pace with her short legs, so his parents walked together at a slower pace. Our baby was due in a week and we hadn't decided on a name yet, so that was our topic of conversation during much of our walking. By the 9th of July, it was decided that if it was a girl, we would name her Juli (however, Jim didn't yet know my intended spelling of the name).

It was the 10th of July – my due date – and even though Dr. Wiens had said it could be *any day, nothing was happening. We may as well go out walking beans again. I had been in the habit of taking a nap every day since my doctor's appointment. When Dr. Wiens had said, "Soon", I pressed him to get his idea of what "soon" meant. He smiled and answered, "I'll probably see you at the hospital before your appointment next Tuesday". That's all it took for me to decide this baby will come by the due date. I decided to take a nap every day so I was ready. We didn't spend all day in the field on the 10th because I took a nap. Jim, on the other hand, hadn't had a nap. When we went to bed he fell asleep right away but I just couldn't get comfortable. I dozed but then would wake up uncomfortable and it was only 11pm. It suddenly dawned on me that my discomfort was coming and going in waves. I lay in bed, wide awake now, trying to figure out if these were contractions. Yes, they were definite contractions now and they were coming every 5 minutes. We had no health insurance at that time so I decided we would wait until after midnight to go to the hospital. Little did I know that we could have waited until after midnight* of the next night!! I woke Jim up after midnight when the contractions started coming more often. Not knowing how soon this baby might come, we called the hospital and they said to come in. I was excited now. I thought we would soon have a baby.

How long had it been since a baby had lived in this house? Who was the first baby in this home? It is certainly likely that the first children to live in this house were actually born in the house. Perhaps Jacob Nickel's children were all born in this house. At that time, women were assisted by a midwife (who was usually a woman in the community who was good with helping with the birth process), while family members or friends took care of the other children and household tasks. As my mother-in-law described to me, during the 1920s and 1930s it was very normal for the babies to be born at home. After the birth, mothers were encouraged to stay in bed for 10 days. "By the time we laid around for 10 days, we really were weak," she said. I was aware that it had been many years since there was a baby in the house. Aaron Becker's boys were *close to Jim's age, but they were not living here until their boys were a little older. Pete Nickel's children may have been the last babies in the house, perhaps 30 years ago. It was time for baby sounds to bounce off these walls again.*

We had come to the hospital early Sunday morning, but the process was going slow. By Sunday afternoon, the contractions were much stronger and were wearing me out. On Sunday evening Dawn & Orv stopped by the hospital to check on how things were coming. Jim was talking with them outside in front of the hospital as Calvin Remple came driving by. He hollered out of his car window, "Hey, has your wife had her kid yet?" Jim called back, "Are you married yet?"

Our little girl was finally born Monday morning, July 12, 1976 at 7:30am. I had never felt such a sense of awe. I couldn't believe this new little life was part me and part Jim. We basked in our joy as we watched our little Juli Suzanne in the warming bed. Later, Jim promised he would never make me do that again. I thought it really wasn't that bad, if I *could just finally go to sleep. By Friday I was very anxious to get out of the hospital. The cost for our baby was under $1000. The doctor bill for the prenatal, delivery and visits after the birth was $250 and the hospital cost $666 for 6 days for both me and baby. Is it any surprise we didn't need health insurance back then?*

We brought our new little bundle of joy home on Friday morning. A little newborn crib that both I and my mother had slept in as babies was awaiting Juli's little body in our bedroom. I was so glad to be back home. My mom had come and made meals for the day. Mom and I were sitting in the living room in the early afternoon when Juli started to cry again. I asked my mom, "Why does she cry? She's fed, she's changed, she's burped, what's wrong?" My mom answered, "Sometimes babies just cry". I wasn't so sure I was ready to deal with that. If I was being called on to do something, I wanted to know what to do. After four years of only Jim and I in the house, this was a strange, new arrangement. I felt very unsure of myself during those first few weeks of having someone totally dependent on me 24 hours a day. One

day I said to Jim, "I have to get out of here", so
we took off in our Roadrunner with Juli lying on
my lap (no baby car seats in those days - in fact,
if I went for a drive to town to get groceries, I
just laid baby Juli on a pillow on the front seat).
We drove around the neighborhood and out
and about on roads I hadn't been on for a long
time. Ah, life was back to normal – I was out for
a drive with my boyfriend!

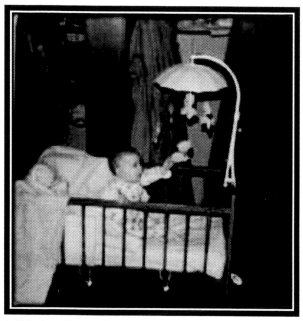

Juli in her first crib which was sitting in front of our closet in our bedroom for the first 5 months

We took great joy in our little Juli. The walls of this old house were filled with love (and sometimes crying and frustration). Days turned into weeks, weeks turned into months, and our little girl grew and developed as any baby does, except that we thought she was the brightest and most beautiful child ever! She certainly learned early how to pull herself up on the crib rails. By the time she was 5 months old, we knew we had to get her into a crib with higher sides. It seemed like a good time to move her into a room farther away from us now too. We set up a new crib in the corner of the living room.

Winter was upon us again and with it came winds that would blow out our heaters during the night. It didn't take long for the bedroom to cool off with no heat. Juli was snuggled below heavy quilts in her crib in the living room, but still she got cold and would wake up. I'd bring her to bed with us and nurse her and change her diaper in our bed to keep warm. We only used cloth diapers with rubber pants to keep the wet from getting to the clothes. I didn't want to get back up in the cold

*and carry the wet diaper back to the diaper pail,
so I laid it on our linoleum floor until morning.
Juli would sleep between us and stay nice and
warm. In the morning we all moved to the
kitchen where it was warmer. Juli sat in her
swing all bundled up, while I cleaned up the
house. The first time I picked up the wet diaper
from our bedroom floor and found it frozen to
the floor only reinforced what we already knew
– our bedroom was the coldest room in the
house. Now we had a little one anxious to crawl
and move around but the floor was rarely more
than 55 degrees in winter even when the
heaters worked. Our adventures in a cold house
weren't much fun anymore. On windy days, it
was hard to find a warm place in the house.
One day when Jim came in for supper, I let out
all the frustration that had been building up in
me throughout the day as I had tried to get
some work done in the kitchen with only the
kitchen heater working. Juli was cold and fussy
so I had the bright idea of moving her crib into
the bathroom and using the electric heater to
keep that one little room warm. The idea of
keeping the room warm worked quite well, but*

having Juli stay in that little room with the door closed and mommy on the outside was utter disaster. Moving the crib into the bathroom was an accomplishment by itself. It allowed just enough room for me to squeeze past and sit down on the toilet seat with my knees touching the crib. I got Juli's toys all arranged and she seemed to be playing happily so I squeezed back out and left her alone to play with her toys. Happiness without mommy in the room only lasted about 10 minutes the first time and much less as the day wore on. My only chance to leave the bathroom without a screaming baby was when she had fallen asleep. It was no fun nursing a baby while sitting on a toilet seat so the next session I grabbed her heaviest blanket and sat in the rocking chair, but then the chill air moved in on my quiet body and soon I was the one who was cold and fussy. It seemed like the day wore on forever and I got nothing done. That evening Jim managed to get the heaters lit again and we started to seriously discuss the possibility of building a new house.

Juli loved taking a bath. The walls in the bathroom needed a lot of work.

A new problem that we were encountering in the kitchen that winter was the issue of our water pipes freezing. We didn't have a lot of snow cover, but we had a lot of wind. Every fall to prepare our house for winter we stacked straw bales around the foundation of the kitchen and dining room since the water pipes had to run in the crawl space between the floor and the ground. Once the first snow fell, we shoveled snow on top of and around the bales and it usually kept the crawl space insulated enough to keep our pipes from freezing. When we didn't have enough snow to cover the bales or foundation our pipes would begin to freeze. Jim would drag the Knipco heater to the west side of the kitchen, pull the bales away, open the door to the crawl space and blow warm air in until the pipes thawed. The risk of letting the pipes freeze was the possibility that they might burst, so our secondary trick was to let the water slowly dribble so there was a little water running through the lines.

The winter was convincing us that this house was no longer meeting our needs with a baby added to our family. Our plan for a new house was taking shape. We began to study new house plans. At that time there were a number of companies that sold a "precut house". They had various floor plans with the lumber all cut to size so the house could be framed quickly. Jim was drawn to the company called "Waconia Homes" because he liked their triple pane windows and some of the other building specs that seemed to make the house constructed better. When it came to the floor plan and design of the house, our old ordinary house had given us a good feel for what we wanted in a floor plan. It was important to us that the kitchen and dining room be on the east side of the house to face the yard. We liked having the laundry on the main floor and wanted a provision for that. We wanted an open feeling between the dining/kitchen/living room areas. Most of all, our old house had convinced us that it would be so nice to have the luxury of a second bathroom off of our bedroom. My dad took our ideas and drew a floor plan for us that we gave to Waconia Homes and let them come up with the exact room dimensions and building specs.

Chapter 8

It was hard to believe that this pile of burning rubble in front of us is all that is left on this yard of our old house. We were quite sure that we had made history in that house with our plans for building a new house. We don't think anyone else who had lived in the house had planned to abandon it completely and build a new one, even though there were probably many plans made to remodel or build an addition. The thought began to enter our minds of what we would do with our old house once we had a new one built, but we would think about that later.

The plans were all made, the spot for the new house was plotted out, and on April 9, 1977 my dad came with his backhoe and dug the hole for the basement of our new house. Everything began to move very quickly. Jim and his dad worked on the sewer lines, while my dad installed the septic tank. The footings were poured and then one weekend in May Jim's cousins, Paul and Dale Wiens, came from Rochester and set up forms for the basement walls, poured the cement walls, and took their forms back home. Shortly after, the "house" (all the lumber, doors and windows, etc.) was delivered. A crew came in and put up the frame in 11 days. Suddenly, our yard took on a new look. A sleek new rambler sat at an angle just to the north behind the old house. What had been the focal point on the yard now stood looking like just an ordinary old farm house. All the excitement was moving and changing behind that tall structure.

The new house is on the right and the old house is on the left. The old garage and clothes hanging on the clothesline are in the middle.

Our crops were all planted by the time the frame was up, and now it was time for us to get busy working on the part of the house we planned to do ourselves. We shingled the roof, put in the plumbing and electric wiring, installed the subfloor, put up the sheetrock, and built the two sets of steps to the basement; all with gracious help from Jim's dad and brothers, and my dad.

We also had a lot of help from little Juli, who spent many days playing in our unfinished new house. She had learned to walk at 10 months – probably because the floors were too cold to crawl on. She would often take off with a hammer, tape measure, or square. We would look and look and then realize Juli must have taken it. When asked where the tool was, many times she could show us where she had put it, but sometimes she had been so busy "helping" that she forgot.

It was exciting and challenging to make all the decisions as to how we wanted this or that done. There were so many choices to make. We planned our kitchen cabinets and *had them custom made. We choose all the flooring for the whole house on one rainy day in October. We picked out the bricks for the fireplace, choose paint colors, and bought all of our lighting.*

The spring, summer, and fall flew by and suddenly we were back to winter in our cold, old house. The bedroom heater never worked anymore and Jim didn't try to fix it. He spent his time getting our new house ready.

We realized it would be January before we could move in. The water pipes in the kitchen were freezing a lot this winter. We had no hot water in the kitchen anymore during the last weeks in our old house. We had to get it from the bathroom, or heat it up on the stove. It was time to move!

"Look mom, I found all the good stuff!" Juli in our bright green kitchen cabinets

Moving day finally arrived and I was sick. We had help from family and church carrying our furniture and other boxes. I barely felt well enough to stay in the new house and tell everyone where to put the furniture.

The next day as I felt better I went back over to the bare house that had been our honeymoon "cottage", our winter adventure, our "think tank" where we came up with goals and plans for the future, and the place we started a family. I looked over the bare walls and floors. I knew this was not the first time this house had been emptied of its contents, but I also knew that this time would be the last time. Was I being too sentimental to shed tears, knowing that in the future I would no longer be able to go back and look at these walls and think of all the memories we had in this house? I had a brand new house waiting for me just steps away. It was a warm house with hot water in the kitchen, carpet on the floors, windows without waves; a house perfectly positioned to see anyone coming on the yard from any window in the front of the house. Surely I didn't need this big eyesore to keep my memories alive, and yet as I walked through each room and thought of our time here, I harbored only feelings of thankfulness that we were able to enjoy our time within these walls. Yes, my memories would continue without the building remaining, but could someone else use this building, or at least part of it? We hadn't had time to think about the future of our old house, but now that we no longer needed it, the time was here. Jim walked in and I asked, "So what are we going to do with this house?" His response included, "There's good lumber in this house." That settled it. We would try to see if someone else could use the whole house or something from it.

In spring we prepared an ad to run in the Mountain Lake Observer. It read:

This old shack has got to go! Tear it down, move it, our old house has got to go. Contact Jim Dick at 427-2082.

We wondered what kind of response we might get. After it came out in the paper, we heard comments from neighbors and friends but none of them were really interested. However, it only took a few days and we received a phone call asking if we were serious about giving the house away because he knew of someone who might want it. A few days *later, as Jim was skreeting the cement for the garage floor, he looked up and there stood Pete Nickel. It turned out that Pete and Alvina had retired from mission work in Alaska and had a small house in Mt. Lake that he wanted to add on to. He was interested in taking lumber from our old house for his project. We were thrilled that someone else could use the house and even more thrilled that it was a former occupant and someone who really needed the lumber. Pete and Alvina started slowly tearing the house apart. We would walk over and visit with them sometimes or help them other times. Pete loved to tell stories. I could tell that his memories of the times they lived in this house were revived as he worked. One day as we were visiting he said, "Come upstairs, I have something to show you". We went upstairs where some of the wall and ceiling were pulled apart. "See that lumber" he said, "that was from the house / barn combination that stood on this yard". What a rare coincidence this seemed to be, that the lumber from a previous home was used to build this house and now the lumber from this house would be used in another house. I was fascinated with the fact that the house we had lived in had lumber in it from a previous house. We wondered aloud when the house / barn had been built but Pete could only generally assume it was the late 1800s. I was curious as to how old this house was. Pete thought and decided it must have been built between 1907 and 1910, which would have meant that Peter Friesen had been the one to build the house. Shortly after building it (in 1914) he sold the 160 acres to Jacob Nickel. Pete enjoyed talking about the house. Another day we came over and helped Pete take up the hardwood floor from the living room. He had opened the plaster on the wall in the living room and showed us how the builders had used newspaper to help insulate the walls. We were finding out many interesting stories about our old house. We were ready to help and young and energetic, but Pete needed a break, so we all took a break from the work for a while. Perhaps more than a break, he was needing to share how the Lord had worked in his life as a testimony not only to what God can do, but to share the peace and contentment of a life yielded to God's call. We moved into the old kitchen, the room I had wanted to tear off and start over. Pete said, "This room has such special memories for me." By now this room held special memories for us also. I thought of a romantic kiss, tears over a burnt meal, a baby's giggle and joy at finding the pots and pans, sleeping on a mattress in this room during a snowstorm; so many moments frozen in time. Pete continued, "I felt the Lord asking me to be a missionary. I prayed and told Him, 'But Lord, I want to be a farmer, and besides that I don't want to go someplace far away that I don't know anything about. I know how to farm. I have a family. I want to keep them safe – in a place that I can take care of them. I don't want to learn another language. You might ask me to do difficult things. My family might get sick and die.' I had all these excuses for God to just leave me alone." He paused and looked at us, "You see, I was just running from God." He paused, "And I got sick. I mean I got really sick. I could hardly get the chores done. I could barely stand up." He looked around the kitchen and pointed to the south wall. "There was a chimney on that wall. I remember the day so well that I stood by the Mea Grope (a German word for the huge rendering kettle that you cooked the animal fat into lard and cracklings) with my hands on the sides of it like this." He positioned himself slightly stooped over, head bowed, with his hands down flat on an imaginary counter. "I finally told the Lord, 'God, I don't care what you do with me. I am so sick. I'm willing to do whatever you want and go where ever you want me to go.' And you know, from that moment on I began to feel the strength come back in my body. It wasn't long before I felt completely normal." Pete shook his finger as he continued, "But you know, I never forgot what I had told God that day. I was willing to go anywhere. And do you know where He sent me? To the best place on earth – Alaska! And we had the best years there. And to think that I had fought against His will so hard and here He had the most wonderful plan for me. Sometimes we think we are willing to trust God, but we aren't willing to just let Him take over, we still have to do what we want. We just don't trust that when we give everything over to Him that He will give us such joy and peace and happiness."*

I could hardly believe there was such a wonderful story to go along with that old dirty chimney. Who knew all the stories that this kitchen held? Only these four walls; and they would soon be gone forever. . . . .

*The fire was not much more than smoke and embers now. Why did it make me so sentimental to see the remains of the shell of the house completely gone? It had served many families well, but the time had come to replace it. Life would go on and carry many more joys and tears within our new dwelling. Perhaps every house that becomes a home and holds dear memories of a family's love, laughter and tears, needs a tribute. Perhaps that is true even if it is . . . . . **just an ordinary house.***